FOR THE
MOMENT

To/ Anna
Thank you so
much for your
support.

FOR THE
MOMENT
CHARNJIT GILL

I hope you find
it healing!

Lots of love
From
Charnjit
x x x x *atmosphere press*

Anna
Thank you so
much for your

I hope you find

Lots of love

DREAMS

I water my dreams with tears
It's the only way it makes things clear
It makes you realise what you hold dear
To scare you out of your comfort zone and conquer your fears
Life runs at its own speed- we're not changing gears
You listen to everything, but no one hears
An insult is a compliment with a jeer
An admiring look with a leer
Does it push you further or near?
Success in its own time, it's just a matter of years

*

Arrest my eyes for what I have seen
Injustice of every kind and the world's broken dreams
The world is too dark for it to be cleaned
Everyone's just mean
Now it's just negativity that fills our screen
It's never been harder to be a teen
We've forgotten what it's like to feel serene
It's all tearing apart now especially at the seams

SLEEP

Every night we arrive at the borders of sleep
But the mind won't let you cross
It's frustrating
Especially when we know it's so straightforward

*

Sometimes all you can do is lie in bed and hope to fall asleep
before you fall apart
Then when you wake up, consider it a fresh start
Sometimes life gives you a jumpstart
Which means it's time to restart
This time we're going to take part
Not be a spare part
Either way, you're still a work of art

OPEN UP

While I'm asleep, I hope my disappointments talk to my dreams
I hope my heartbreak speaks to my habits
I hope my goals talks to my game plan
I hope my sadness talks to my satisfactions
I hope my losses talks to my laughter
I hope the abyss talks to my art
I hope my experience talks to my emotions
I hope my ignorance talks to my inquisitions
I hope my capabilities talk to my creativity
I hope my uncertainties talk to my understanding
I hope my rejections build a rapport
I hope my memories speak to the margins of my mind and tell it
    to open up

CAPABILITY

We nurse our dreams in the darkness
Reality brings too much to light
Hold onto our hopes
We care about our capabilities

SUNRISE

The sunrise, of course, doesn't care if we watch it or not
It will keep on being beautiful, even if it's no one bothers to look
    at it
It's nature's hack
To change our outlook

SET

The sun doesn't set
We do
We set about to do things
But we experience setbacks
We set our eyes on something else
Then we end up setting fire to everything else
We try to settle in
But something always sets us off
We set out
To set sail
Only to realise that it was a set up

DETERMINATION

Wake up with determination
Go to bed with satisfaction
Wait until you see life's reaction....

*

A smile is an expression of an epiphany
The moment you realise something
The moment you recognise something
The moment you identify something
Or someone

CLARIFY

Clarify your vision
Plan with precision
Don't take anything as given
Make it your personal mission
And it will always have ignition

*

Have a vision
That goes beyond sight
Insight
Foresight
Hindsight
Tunnel vision to the future

PURPOSE

Until you find your purpose
You feel worthless
But maybe that's the purpose
So, when you do find it
You know it was worth it
So, dig deep
Don't just scratch the surface

*

We search for meaning in the meaningless
Because we think, it is redeeming us
That our attachments are leaving us
And our purpose is leading us
It's teaching us

*

Purpose is an incredible alarm clock
It unlocks your ability
Enough to wake you up

CHALLENGE

I challenge my limits
I live all my years in a single minute
Matrix world- we're all falling digits
I tried life on for size and saw how it fitted
It's genuine, original- there's no time for gimmicks
It's not about what you give but what you do with what you're given
Some people mess up and you can't help but grimace
For all the pain and suffering caused- it's a tough image
They say imitation is the biggest form of flattery, but we don't
      have any mimics
We need to keep moving- just pivot
That's it keeps going- that's the spirit
We're all ready and set to go – we bought the ticket
The passengers looking around are far from timid
Hope you enjoyed your stay- it was nice to visit
People and memories are more than vivid
Let the mind exhibit
What the body inhibits

ADVENTURE

Boldly accept life's challenge and adventure
It's what makes it a living force
A course of challenges
A source of struggles
Enforcing emotions
Having remorse about regrets

OPPONENT

I've closed too many doors to know which ones to open
I've seen too many mirrors to know which ones are broken
I've seen too many options to know which one I've chosen
I've seen too many methods to know which one is coping
I've seen too many distractions to know which one to focus
I've been melted too many times to know what it feels to be
    frozen
I've won too many bronzes too know which one is golden
I've seen too much hope to know what it feels hopeless
I've seen too many memories to know which ones to capture the
    moment
I've been too still to know motion
I've been too blind to notice
I've seen too much water to know an ocean
I've seen too many adverts to know a slogan
I've read too many words to know which ones are spoken
I've seen too much possessions to knows which ones are stolen
I've seen too many threads to know which ones are woven
I've seen too many atheists to know devotion
I've been too heartless to know emotion
I've been too friendly to know that I am my only opponent

*

It's not about being whole
It's about staying whole
That's the goal
But it's only a matter of time before we start picking holes
Making mountains out of molehills
Being whole is good for the soul
Otherwise, the broken pieces take its toll

TALKING TO YOURSELF

We tell ourselves not to give up when we've had enough
We tell ourselves it's not worth the risk but life's calling our bluff
We tell ourselves to keep calm when all we do is huff and puff
We tell ourselves that life will be a smooth ride
Then why are we having such a rough time?
We fed ourselves these lies until we're fed up
We tell ourselves to stay young but grow up
We tell ourselves that we'll have it made but the truth is we're
    making it up
We ask ourselves what we must show for it, but we don't answer
    because we don't want to be shown up
We tell ourselves to shut people out, but we just want to tell them
    to shut up
We tell ourselves to get things done
Because we don't want to become undone
We tell ourselves that we can become whatever we want
If the obstacles are overcome

CHARACTER

Every personality has an arc
Everyone wants to leave their mark
A flicker, a flame, a spark

*

Your personality is your personal reality
Made up of what you think and feel
All the emotional intensity and enthusiasm

MIND-SET: TIRED OF THINKING

We become tired of thinking about the things we haven't done
    rather than feeling satisfied with what we have done
Like preparing for things in the long run
Or helping a loved one
Becoming someone
Being there for everyone

*

Create a mind-set that is immune to doubt and uncertainty
Where everything you do is done perfectly
As though it's done purposely

TRUE TO YOU

You are deserving because of who you are not what you do
Out of the many, you are one of the few
That treats the old like the new
Because of what you've been through
Because you stayed true
True to you
You see through what others don't see at all

*

Whatever you reveal
You heal
Because you say, how you feel
To see what's real
And make it ideal

BOLD

You never know how bold you should be
Too little- not brave enough
Too much- that's daring enough

DRINK

We all drink from the same fountain
But push each other going up the same mountain
They say it's not competitive but there is counting
The ones who taught you to swim are drowning
So, can you blame them if there's still doubting?

★

Everybody wants to shine but no one wants to polish
Everyone wants the truth, but no one wants to be honest

FREQUENCY

We give too many people the power to lower our vibrations
Stand true to your own frequency

*

Whatever life throws at you, even if it hurts you
Just be strong and fight through it
Remember strong walls shake but never collapse
The cracks let the light through

SHY

Shy people notice everything, but they aren't noticed
The more they see, the more they are out of focus

★

We don't want to be looked at
We want to be seen
Acknowledged

★

Some people are shy
Some people are so shy that they stay inside their shell
If you want to talk to them, you don't get them to climb out
You have to climb in
That's how you find their pearls
Pearls of wisdom

LEVER

The forgotten ones are a lever
They have a power or influence
That can operate anything
But people use them as leverage

CARING

I like people that show they care
In this cold-hearted world
It's nice to know that someone's out there

TOUCH SCREEN

In a touch screen world where everything is on display
Zoom in or zoom out
Layers upon layers
Of thin space
Covered in fingerprints
It's nice that someone can feel what you're saying
Tap your heart
Pat your back
Stir your mind
Trace your words

SILENCE

If silence is so loud, can you hear it?
If it's so deafening, can you bear it?
Are you afraid? Do you fear it?
Does the silence drive you mad or do you steer it?
Does it rip you apart or do you tear it?
Does it dress itself or do you wear it?

★

We break the silence
Knowing that no words could ever fix it
Tight lips
Lead to internal scripts
And rips
Line skips
Freudian slips
Words at the tip of your tongue
That just trip
And whip you into silence

TITLE: MUTE

We've all got problems
We all have the ability to solve them
Even if it takes some time
You can ask for help
We all need it
Sometimes you just need someone to listen
Really hear you out
Not tell you what to do
But ask you the right questions so that you have the answers to
People can tell you to move on
But you know it's not easy
People will leave you
Fact
Having someone sit with you
Optional
You might argue mandatory
But when you're taking an inventory of your life
It's not as simple as it seems
Love yourself
Trust that you will work it out

*

Sometimes we turn the volume up on our problems
We turn the volume down on our solutions
We need to mute to find a resolution
A conclusion
For improvement

ONIONS

Humans are like onions
We peel the layers of bravado
The walls of defence
To get to who we really are
And when we do- the honesty makes us cry

FALL

People are not rain or snow
They do not look beautiful when they fall
The humiliation makes them want to curl up into a ball
Who can they turn to?
Who can they call?
It's like being the first guest in a hall
It's the way a big room can make you feel so small
It doesn't matter how short or tall
Embarrassment puts your back against the wall

GAME CHANGER

Life is a game
You are a player
You play
And get played

⋆

The world is already full of players
The game has already got levels and layers
But it's not the type of game where you can pull in a favour
Not from family, a friend or a neighbour
This is a game between givers and takers
For the people that wait and the waiters

DEFEAT

Sometimes defeat is the best outcome
Because it changes your outlook

*

I look forward to disappointments
They are poignant

WEIGHT

Weight is your enemy
It holds back your destiny
Endlessly
We rely on it heavily
But we use it messily
We think its weaponry
But it contains our complexities
Because of our dependency
Especially when we tell ourselves
We will use it eventually
But we don't- it just increases its expectancy
But we don't think about longevity
Ask yourself – is it a necessity?
Could you use it successfully?

SILVER LINING

Don't miss the silver lining because you were expecting gold
Don't let go of the cloud because it's cold
You might not like the hand you've been dealt but don't fold

LOST

When you feel lost, take yourself into your heart
Follow its rhythm
Follow its beat
Follow the blood flow from your head to your feet
We'll retrace the places your heart goes and the people that you
    meet
The journey might not be straightforward or neat
Where did you leave your heart?
When did you give it?
Who did you give it to?
What did they do with it?
Why did they have it?
How did they treat it?
Not the way that you wanted them to.
Did they break it?
So, let's go around your heart and pick up the pieces
We can fix it together and it'll be like its brand new
You didn't lose your heart
You didn't find your heart
You found you
You made yourself into what you wanted to

*

Lost is the place where you go to find yourself
Where are you going?
I'm going to get lost
I'm going to find myself at any cost

SELF RELIANCE

Self-reliance is the greatest art
Because it shows your heart
All its parts

★

No one ever stays
No one ever will
No one is supposed to
You've got to do this on your own
Pick your own bones
Sit on your own throne
It's how you strengthen your own backbone

PRICELESS

Invest in yourself
It pays the best interest
Every step is a dividend
It's priceless

FINANCE

If money doesn't grow on trees, why do banks have branches?
If time is money, then I'll take my chances
Payment is upfront- I take advances
We live in a world that wants expansion
Especially when it comes our finances
Whatever the circumstance is

UNIVERSE

When you think you know all the answers, the universe changes
    all the questions
When you think you've finished learning, the universe changes
    the lessons
When you think you know where you're going in life, the
    universe changes directions

*

The hardest thing in life is to know which bridge to cross and
    which to burn
Which tables to sit at and which to turn
Which lessons to give and which to learn

ATTENTION

Give attention to opportunities
It gives success its immunity

DISENGAGED

We don't fail because of incompetence
But because we are not engaged
We fail because we feel caged
Unable to fulfil our potential
We become enraged
It is beyond us
We feel outraged
We don't want to admit it
But we're afraid
That success comes with time
Now it's delayed
It doesn't matter how much we change
Sometimes the results remain unchanged
Which is why we are disengaged

BLIND

Failure and success are both blind
Success only sees itself
Failure sees nothing else

EFFECT

We don't fear success
We don't fear failure
We fear neither
We fear the effect of it

DETACHED

Sometimes we're so detached from what we experience
That it's hard to use that experience

*

Life doesn't give you an explanation
We give it one

LIVING

Giving up is harder than trying
Choosing is harder than buying
Smiling is harder than crying
Being honest is harder than lying
Being confident is harder than being shy
Losing is harder than tying
Defying is harder than complying
Accepting is harder than denying
Living is harder than dying

*

Break the foundation of life and build a living
Keep digging

PASSION

What happens when your passion passes away?
It's up to the passengers to remind the driver, why they set off in
    the first place
Sometimes the chase loses its thrill
Where you must face up to the reality
Some people do it with grace
Others with hate
But you set up your own pace
Sometimes the race doesn't seem worth running
You can feel like a waste of space
But passion is beyond a bookcase
It embraces you

INNOVATION

Failure drives innovation
Because it brings everything into formation
If success is at the top, then failure is the foundation
That's why success gets a standing ovation
Everyone has ideas but it's about application
Success is an aspiration
That's why it needs concentration
Contemplation
If success is a declaration then failure is defamation
Success is a journey not a destination
It has many stations
Failure is success in need of motivation
Navigation
Transformation

*

We emulate the result not the process
That's why failure leads to success
Go ahead
But don't forget
You get the result with the mind-set
Sometimes it feels like it makes no sense
The process is the outlet
Prepare to progress
So, the results can refresh
You can get what you want with no regrets
But I have one request
Once you've emulated the results, make sure you reset

ARMOUR

Giving up is easier than trying harder
But rejection makes an invincible armour

*

Rejection tests whether you are serious about your dreams
There are times when rejection tears you at the seam
But acceptance is in your genes
Once you've been accepted once, it will be a domino effect
Like a machine

BOUNCE BACK

The harder you fall, the higher you bounce
Success is measured in weight by the ounce
Get ready to pounce
It's time to announce
That you won so many points– we lost count

★

Success is the sum of small efforts
Repeated day in and day out
It removes failure's doubts
Helps you become devout
Consider it a workout

★

If you are constantly improving, you are winning
Every inning
Because the end is a new beginning
You never know what change is bringing
On what foundation its building
To find out the depth of character you must keep digging
Because success is fitting
You can't take it as a given
If you're not giving anything
Take the hit and keep hitting
You were born kicking
It's a sign of living

★

When you're at the top, it's easier for success to fall on you
But failure wants to fall through
To tell you that you haven't paid your dues
That you're screwed
But its view is slightly skewed
Only success sees the breakthrough
The debut

The preview
So, you know how to pursue
And die as much as you live up to

STRUGGLE IS FREE FOR ALL

Stop trying to skip the struggle
This is where character is built
Embrace it
Learn from it
Grow from it
Hard work is about reaping what you sow
Just go with it
Otherwise, failure will drag you in tow

*

When you feel like you're at the end of your wits
Don't quit
When you feel like your life is in bits
It's a good thing
It shows you how everything fits
It's not always about the times that you hit
It's the times that you miss
Too many people live according to a checklist
Education, work, marriage, kids
But just when you think that life seems straightforward
It shows you its twists
How easily you can fall
Fall into the abyss
You'll be surprised at how much that experience is pure bliss
Because all that reminds you to do is listen to the pulse in your wrist

*

Your struggles will be admired only after you become successful
Then those lessons seem helpful
Because you've achieved a different level
Where others settled
You didn't give in until the success was special
You became a vessel
That you often wrestled with
Knowing it's essential

People are more judgemental
When they don't see the potential
At the time, it seems resentful which they become regretful of
Once you achieve success, people can be resentful of the result
But disrespect the struggle
By that point, you've already achieved the monumental
So everything else is uneventful

HARD WORK

The harder you work
The luckier you get
Go against the odds
And have the highest bet
The more you earn
The lower the debt
The wider the horizon
The wider you spread the net
Success comes in small portions
You've got a lot left

*

Sometimes your attitude is more important than your ability
Your strength is more important than your stability
Your tactics are more important than your talent
Your focus is more important than your flexibility

SUCCESS

We see success
Not the struggle
We see the biscuits
Not the crumbles
We see the animals
Not the jungle
We see the fists
Not the knuckles
We see the rain
Not the puddles
We see fire
Not the rubble
We see plants and flowers
Not the shovel
We see the train
Not the tunnel

UNSTOPPABLE

It's not about being perfect
It's about being unstoppable
Overcoming every obstacle
Making the impossible- possible
It's about being phenomenal

*

When the odds are impossible
The rationale is laughable
We don't waver
We don't wince
Slay
Overcome problems
Crush
Save the day

FIGHT BACK

Fighting back is part of our existence
It keeps us consistent
Insistent
Determined to win
Adamant that you can make it happen
Unrelenting effort
Tenacious energy
Unfaltering in your investment
Unwavering schedules
Demanding your discipline
Pressing your power
Firm principles
Assertive action
To receive the right result

Persistent
Persevering your potential
Purposeful principles
Single mind-set
Tireless training
Patient with the process
Daily diligent
Constant comebacks
Nonstop narrative
Steady steps
Uninterrupted focus
Incessant ideals
Endless empathy
Sustained sacrifices
Lingering luck

Resistant
To defeat with damage
Impervious to failure
Proof against power
Unaffected by anything
Immune to influence

Waterproof tears
Opposed to opposition
Averse to others ability
Hostile to bad habits
Against adversity
Anti-affliction

Prize

Sometimes the harder you fall
The stronger you rise
The bigger the prize

TOUGH

Our toughest times can bring out a gentler side
Where we are more tender
More loving
More caring
More appreciative

So, we stop taking people for granted

★

Toughness is in the soul and spirit
Not in muscles
It's in the hustle
In the struggle
In the trouble

CIRCLE

Keep your circle pure, sacred and small
So that there is always someone to catch you when you fall
They can help you kick the curve balls
Pick you up at down falls

UNCOMFORTABLE

You are growing when you feel uncomfortable
It's an acknowledgement of change
There has been a challenge and you have embraced it
You are growing when you see things you didn't see before
Problems don't seem as puzzling
Solutions seem simple
You understand things better
You'll be different
You're growing when you master your own service
Everything becomes more positive
There is a change in behaviour
Change in dynamics
You are growing when you gain clarity
Once you have it, you crave more of it
Explore it
You are growing when you enjoy the journey
Rather than reaching the destination

DIRECTION

Direction is more important than speed
Generosity is more important than greed

STAND OUT

We want to stand out without overshadowing others
We want to blend in without fading away
We don't want to betray who we really are
We embrace
The escape
It's hard to explain
Bu it heals the heartache
Because mistakes like to parade
Either they remain
Or are replaced
Which is something to celebrate
To appreciate

LISTEN

Listen to your own voice before you listen to anyone else's
Understand your thoughts
Understand why you feel the way you do
Find the answers inside yourself
Find yourself before you get lost
Save yourself
Heal yourself
Leave people behind
Walk away
Move on
Get comfortable being alone
You aspire to live a different life
So, fight for it
No one knows you better than yourself
Everything will make sense

1%

To be part of the 1%
You do what the other 99% won't
You do what the other 99% don't

IN BETWEEN

I'm in that awkward in between stage
Where I'm not a caterpillar or a butterfly
Where I'm not saying hello or even goodbye
When I don't know when to laugh or when to cry
Where I'm not living but I can't die
In between the lows and the highs
In between the lies in honesty and the truth in all the lies
Not confident not shy
Where I'm neither keeping it together nor stopping it from going
    awry
Where I'm not abiding or defying
Where I'm not accepting or denying
Where I'm not going or getting by
Where I'm not bringing justice or trying to justify
This life

RUSH

You'll never make more mistakes
than when you're in a rush to solve a problem
This is where the mighty
have fallen

REST

Embrace the concept that rest, recovery and reflection are essential
  parts of progress
They help you stay blessed
It allows you to assess the situation
Express how you feel
Without having to impress
You can obsess over it
Ultimately, it's part of the process
Of success
For failure's repossess

HOME

Home is the centre of life
It is the refuge from work
Home is where we can be ourselves
Out of the house, we are someone else
Home is our roots
From which we grow and blossom
As children, we imagine and play
As teenagers, we retreat
As adults, we want to settle
We look forward to coming home after a long day
You can tell a lot about a person from the house they are raised in
    and the house they live in
When we move, it's only to create replicas of home elsewhere

TEMPORARY

Success comes with temporary defeat and at times failure
The movie of your life will come out soon just watch the trailer
Sometimes you are your own saviour
So, you must watch your own behaviour
Put the time in and the money will come later

WAIT

I don't worry
I wait
I wait to get what I want
What I need
I believe more in myself
And less of everyone else
I keep my faith stronger than my fears
I spend more time at a table than wiping my tears

*

I couldn't wait for success
So, I went ahead without it
Stopped doubting myself
Called on my capabilities
Found failure
Instead of waiting for a handout

STEPS

Feeling successful generates success
It could be from the way you dress
The way you make an educated guess
The way you deal with stress
Or the fact that you love saying 'yes'

★

Success has three steps:
What you have
What you do
What you present

WORKOUT

Success is the sum of small efforts
Repeated day in and day out
It removes failure's doubts
Helps you become devout
Consider it a workout

INSULATE

Success insulates
It covers mistakes
Prevents failure
Isolates influence

SHADOWS

Power, wealth and youth are all shadows
It makes us think that we're the archer when we're really the
    arrow

★

The seeds of your struggle
Plant your power
Grow your genius
Reproduce your resilience
Blossom into your boldness

OBLIVION

Unleash progress, creativity and resilience
Make a difference
Be brilliant
Experience oblivion

*

Progress doesn't move in straight lines
It zigs zags
But we're all expecting an ascending straight line on a graph

BECOMING

Sometimes becoming is better than being
Because it keeps you dreaming
It gives you meaning
It allows you to keep seeking
To keep believing

GROW

Grow where you are planted
Make use of what you're granted

*

Grow, reflect, and flourish
Nourish yourself
So, you don't perish
Do it with courage
Cherish everything
With purpose

TIME

Time is the most valuable thing that we possess
Its supply is limited
So, we must be disciplined
Because the end is imminent
But it feels limitless

★

Time is of the essence
That's just the basics
Of nature
Time is indispensable
Our life is a concentrated extract

FAST LIFE

Life is not too short
We didn't expect it to go so fast

MOVEMENT

Ever since your first ultrasound, every movement is watched
    carefully
Like each one determines your destiny
Sometimes your movement is watched fearfully
Go gracefully
Your heart needs to be in harmony
Every step should be taken sensibly

★

The road ahead stretches out ahead of you
It pulls you closer
It extends its hands
It lengthens the lane
It elongates the exit
It straightens the streets
It sprawls out
Covering the country

ULTIMATE TRUTH

If death is the ultimate truth, is life deceived?
If time is money, why does the day need to be seized?
If common sense is common, why are we so naïve?
If failure is so bad, then why on the path to success is it guaranteed?

AMEND

Amend your life often and ruthlessly
It's your masterpiece
It's the only way you'll be at peace

*

I want you to feel peaceful
Calm
Happy
I hope you're healthy
I hope you stay safe
I hope you become at ease with life

DECORATE

Life is an ambitious piece of art
A moving performance
A real work of fiction
It's a blank canvas of characters
Where the plot pours in
It's a technicolour film
A lulling piece of music

★

Art is how we decorate space
Music is how we decorate time
Love is how we decorate life

SIT POWERFUL

Sit Powerful
Don't sit back powerless
Sit powerful
Leave the world on the edge of its seat
Wondering what you're going to do next
Sit Powerful

GRATEFUL

I'm grateful
I'm happy to be here
Taking one step a time
Going somewhere
I don't need the empty world to fill me
I don't know the right questions to ask
I don't need answers
I don't need to be so hard on myself
We all want to believe they there is something greater for us
No one knows where the road goes
And maybe that's the best thing about it

BIGGER

We are so much bigger than we seem
But the universe makes us small
We are trying
Trying is the point of life
Don't stop trying
There are times we tell ourselves to give up
But we know we're lying
We've got too many loose ends that need tying
We've got to pursue things that are satisfying
Or are terrifying
Life is about fighting
When you're younger, it's about rising
As you get older, it's keeps shining
Keep smiling
Instead of giving into the silence
It's about striving
And surviving
Because death is about timing

MEETINGS AND PARTINGS

Life is made up of meetings and partings
Our greatest meeting is with death
Many nearly meet it
But it's not close enough
Life won't let you finish yet
Our greatest parting is with life
Although we are alive for many years
We only learn to live when we meet love
It's then that we are not living for ourselves
We are living for everyone else
Our loved ones
That's why parting is bittersweet
God needs you back
Because this parting will take you on a different track
Where you'll attend a meeting knowing that you'll never go back

ABOUT ATMOSPHERE PRESS

Atmosphere Press is an independent, full-service publisher for excellent books in all genres and for all audiences. Learn more about what we do at atmospherepress.com.

We encourage you to check out some of Atmosphere's latest releases, which are available at Amazon.com and via order from your local bookstore:

Impression by Charnjit Gill

Poems for the Bee Charmer (And Other Familiar Ghosts), poetry by Jordan Lentz

Flowers That Die, poetry by Gideon Halpin

Through The Soul Into Life, poetry by Shoushan B

Embrace The Passion In A Lover's Dream, poetry by Paul Turay

Reflections in the Time of Trumpius Maximus, poetry by Mark Fishbein

Drifters, poetry by Stuart Silverman

As a Patient Thinks about the Desert, poetry by Rick Anthony Furtak

Winter Solstice, poetry by Diana Howard

Blindfolds, Bruises, and Break-Ups, poetry by Jen Schneider

INHABITANT, poetry by Charles Crittenden

Godless Grace, poetry by Michael Terence O'Brien

March of the Mindless, poetry by Thomas Walrod

In the Village That Is Not Burning Down, poetry by Travis Nathan Brown

Mud Ajar, by Hiram Larew

To Let Myself Go, poetry by Kimberly Olivera Lainez

ABOUT THE AUTHOR

Charnjit Gill has an MA in Creative Writing and a BA in English Literature & Creative Writing. She has been writing and performing poetry for over seven years. Her work has been published in the *London Spoken Word Anthology* 2015-2016 by Gug Press, Typishly, Minerva Rising Press, From Whispers to Roars, KYSO Flash, Ghost City Press, San Fedele Press, Starfeather Publishing, and Poets Choice.

Made in the USA
Monee, IL
05 March 2022

92224537R00059